THE LITTLE BOOK OF CHEFS' TIPS

RICH

THE LITTLE BOOK OF CHEFS' TIPS

RICHARD MAGGS

Absolute Press

First published in Great Britain in 2006 by
Absolute Press
Scarborough House, 29 James Street West
Bath BA1 2BT, England
Phone 44 (0) 1225 316013 **Fax** 44 (0) 1225 445836
E-mail info@absolutepress.co.uk
Web www.absolutepress.co.uk

A catalogue record of this book is available
from the British Library

ISBN 1 904573 38 X

Printed and bound in Italy by Grafica Veneta

'I may not be healthy or wealthy or wise;
I may not have dreamy, mysterious eyes;
I may not wear clothes from a
French fashion book;
But I'm never lonely, for boy, can I cook!'

Anon.

1

When cooking asparagus, this simple trick will preserve its brightest and fullest colour. As with all green vegetables, boil quickly in well-salted water, but **blanch** plenty of **parsley** complete with stalks **in the water** for a few minutes **first.** This chlorophyll-saturated water will then not leach out any of the asparagus' fine colour and flavour.

2

Most people have heard that there's **a nifty chef's way** of using a 'finger test' **to check how well a steak is cooked.** Here's an easy way to remember it: when pressed, if rare, a steak feels like your cheek. If medium to medium-rare, it feels like your chin. If well-done, it feels like your forehead.

3

Butter can burn easily when heated, so,

when shallow frying,

to keep the flavour pure and avoid burning,

use clarified butter instead.

Alternatively, add an equal quantity of a light oil such as groundnut and this will raise the smoking point considerably.

4

When forming meat balls, kebabs, burgers and fishcakes, it is easy for your hands to quickly get into a sticky mess. There is an easy solution – simply

wet your hands

with cold water periodically during the operation

and the mixture won't stick to them.

5

When making casseroles and ragoûts **that have a high fat content,** such as a rich oxtail stew, after cooking, quickly cool and refrigerate. This will enable the removal of the solidified fat the following day before re-heating for serving. The flavour is also often improved with this method.

6

To give cheese sauces definition, add a little English mustard to the sauce. This complements cauliflower especially well. For Welsh rarebit and its cousins, give your sauce piquancy by using a dark beer for a third of the total liquid ingredients.

7

When placing baking parchment onto baking trays before piping choux paste or meringue mixtures, place a small dab of the raw mixture in each corner. Then when the parchment is placed on top it will become anchored safely and won't 'walk' while you are piping.

8

To ripen hard avocados quickly, place with several apples or ripe bananas in a paper bag and close loosely. Leave overnight in a slightly warm room. The captured ethylene gas given off from the fruit will rapidly ripen the avocados. This also works well to ripen bananas.

9

When cooking a large quantity of sausages

on the grill, broiler or barbecue, thread onto two skewers to make 'ladders'. When they are ready to turn, it will take just a few seconds to flip them over.

10

When cutting out pastry shapes, especially when using puff pastry, **always flour the cutter in between use** and stamp down smartly. Resist any temptation to twist the cutter, as this will give misshapen results during baking and also discourage the pastry from rising fully.

11

To calm the heat of chillies

in a curry or other dish if you have been a little heavy-handed,

add the juice of half a lemon

along with the spent lemon half. After five minutes, remove and discard. A little double cream, if necessary, should finally round off the correction.

12

When serving soup, prevent drips from your ladle en route to the soup plate. Fill the ladle and then briefly touch its base on the surface of the soup before taking it to the soup plate. In this way an incomplete drop won't have time to form before the ladle is safely over the centre of the plate.

13

Chefs generally have

no need for a garlic press.

Place a clove on a board and press down with the heel of a large knife and the papery skin will fall off. Then chop finely before adding a little salt and use a scraping motion across the board to form a smooth pulp.

14

To flatten out shortbread mixtures easily n a tin, cover with clingfilm r saran wrap and then press out evenly from e centre. Finally, lightly roll all over using a jar r can to achieve a uniform thickness in seconds efore removing the clingfilm or saran wrap nd baking.

15

For crisp apple or pear wafers to garnish desserts, slice unpeeled and cored fruit thinly on a mandolin. Brush with lemon juice and then with syrup made from 55g (2 oz) sugar dissolved in 30ml (1 fl oz) apple juice. Dry on wire racks in an oven at its coolest setting for 1–2 hours until quite dry and not at all coloured.

16

Lemon juice, when added to anything sweet, **accentuates** its **sweetness,** so is a useful addition instead of leaning exclusively on more and more sugar. For example, try adding a little to some sliced strawberries. It similarly prevents blackcurrants and blueberries from tasting soapy when they are made into mousses and ice creams.

17

To ripen a recalcitrant piece of **Brie or Camembert,**

place on a plate and microwave on Low or Defrost for 15–45 seconds, depending on the size and condition of the cheese. Leave to stand at room temperature for five minutes and then, if necessary, repeat for a further 15 seconds before serving.

18

Root ginger can be easily **peeled using a teaspoon.** Scrape away as when preparing new potatoes, then store as chunks in a polythene bag in the freezer. When needed, it is easy to grate as much as you require from frozen. Use a Microplane if you have one or a fine grater.

19

To divide muffin mixture easily and quickly between moulds or paper cases, **use a mashed potato scoop.** This will also ensure that they all receive an equal amount of mixture and therefore cook at the same rate and to an even size.

20

If a hurriedly-made Hollandaise or Béarnaise **sauce shows signs of curdling,** remove from the heat immediately and add an ice cube. Beat steadily until the mixture stabilises and becomes perfectly smooth. Keep warm in a Pyrex jug in a saucepan of hot tap-water or use a wide-mouth vacuum flask.

21

To produce superb crackling when roasting pork, pat dry with kitchen paper and score deep cuts 6mm ($^{1}/_{4}$ inch) apart using a dedicated craft knife. **Rub in some fine salt** and a little olive oil. Allowing 25 minutes per 450g (1 lb), start in a hot oven at 220°C/425°F/Gas 7. After 40 minutes, continue cooking at 180°C/350°F/Gas 4. Return to a high setting for the final 30 minutes.

22

Juices running clear is a good first check to

ensure that poultry is fully cooked

- further check can be made **by**

'shaking hands' with the legs.

They should be easy to wiggle in their sockets and the thickest portion of the drumsticks should feel tender when pressed.

23

One of the easiest and fastest ways to **prepare a bell pepper** is to cut off the top with the stalk, pull out the seeds as one, then slice and flatten out into a rectangle, removing any remaining pith. It is then easy **to slice or chop in seconds.**

24

To prevent

any danger of **spilling**

uncooked quiche or tart **filling**

when carrying a pastry case to the oven, only half-fill with the mixture. Place on the oven shelf and then pour in the rest of the mixture before closing the door. Whisk before pouring so that any flavouring or seasonings don't get left in the bottom.

25

Once avocado flesh has been exposed to air it will oxidise and discolour. The presence of the stone doesn't prevent this as has sometimes been suggested; **brush with a little lemon juice** or press down clingfilm to exclude air until ready to serve.

26

When poaching fruit, always **add sugar to taste** once the fruit is tender **at the end of cooking,** as it can otherwise toughen the fruit skins. Similarly, when cooking dried pulses, always use plain water or unsalted stock, so that they become tender easily – only add salt at the end.

27

Test if a roast is

properly cooked by sticking a skewer into the centre and leaving it there for a minute. Remove it and gently touch the end against your upper lip. If it feels lukewarm, the meat is **rare.** If the skewer is hot but not too hot to hold against your upper lip, the roast is **medium.** If it's noticeably hot, the meat is **well-done.**

28

When skinning fish fillets, always start at the tail end and **work towards the head.** Place the fillet skin-side down and use a little salt to help you get a good grip. Use a sliding action with the knife almost parallel to the board and the fillet and skin will become quickly separated.

29

Squeeze cooked spinach in a potato ricer to easily press out excess cooking water, **before** returning to a hot pan and **tossing in a little butter,** black pepper and a little freshly grated nutmeg. For an oriental finish, sauté a little garlic and ginger in some oil first and then dress with soy sauce or tai luk.

30

When preparing fruit or vegetables with rounded bases, such as tomatoes and melons, **cut a thin slither from the underside** to make the portion stable on the serving plate. Take care not to cut through to prevent precious juices escaping.

31

To make delicious butters

Maître D'hôtel butters for dressing cooked vegetables, garnishing steaks and for impromptu garlic bread, whiz together herbs and garlic with softened butter in a food processor. Form into a roll, wrap tightly and freeze. Cut into coin shapes before use. Citrus versions using zest and juice are also worth trying.

32

When making Béchamel type sauces, always add hot milk to the roux to **prevent lumps forming.** Reserve a little of the liquid and pour over the sauce once it is made, to prevent a skin forming. Alternatively, place a scrape of butter on the tip of a knife and wipe all over the sauce. Simply whisk in the protective coating before serving.

33

Place a lemon in a hot oven or in the microwave for a couple of minutes before squeezing **to extract the most juice.**

Organic lemons give a far superior flavour and are worth the extra cost. If using the zest first, wash well to remove any wax before using.

34

For a stylish dessert presentation trick, **warm** some bought **brandy snaps** for 3–6 minutes on an oiled tray in a moderate oven. When soft, unroll and drape over ramekins **to form toffee baskets.** When set, use to serve ice cream and sorbets.

35

Roasted garlic is a really useful ingredient and **imparts a deliciously mellow flavour to dishes.** Drizzle a little olive oil over whole heads of garlic with the tops sliced off and bake in a moderately hot oven for 15–20 minutes. When tender, store in a plastic bag in the refrigerator. To use, squeeze out the soft paste on to bread or use in soups and pasta sauces.

36

When poaching eggs, always use the freshest eggs

to prevent them spreading. Fill a non-stick frying pan with hot water 25mm (1 inch) deep. With it barely shivering, slide in the eggs and leave well alone for about four minutes, until perfectly cooked. If you're an apprehensive poacher, cook in an improvised bag made from clingfilm.

37

For the best-ever roast potatoes, try

using a mixture of two kinds of fat. As with shortcrust pastry, this ploy has a magical effect giving the crispiest results.

A great fat combination

is half duck or goose fat with solid vegetable shortening.

38

To keep a cauliflower perfectly white

when boiling, **add** a tablespoon of

lemon juice to the water.

Include a few of the green leaves for extra flavour. If a disagreeable sulphur odour is noticeable, this can be prevented by adding a bay leaf to the water.

39

Microplane graters are universally popular with chefs the world over. If you **grate** the ingredient through the Microplane **towards you,** you will see exactly how much has been produced. To remove all the collected material after grating, use a clean dry pastry brush.

40

To prepare a mango easily,

cut in half lengthways, working with the knife above and below the long oval central stone. Then cut around the middle and separate the two halves. Cut a criss-cross pattern and then turn each half inside out to give a 'hedgehog' effect, making it easy to cut off the exposed flesh into neat cubes.

41

Occasionally,

an unusual ingredient will really complement another flavour.

Add freshly milled black pepper or a few drops of balsamic vinegar to sliced strawberries and leave to macerate for an hour. Also try griddled fresh pineapple with a little chopped chilli.

42

For stunning soup presentation,

try serving two contrasting soups in the same soup plate, choosing ones with a similar consistency. Pour each pan simultaneously into the plate, one on the left and one on the right. You will fill the plate with two D-shapes of soup that will meet in the middle.

43

To revive a slightly stale loaf of bread,

cut off a slice from the 'open' end of the loaf and discard. Hold the loaf, cut-side down, for a few moments under a running cold tap. Then place it in a pre-heated oven at its highest setting for three minutes for warm, crusty bread.

44

Egg whites freeze well. Also, once they have been **frozen,** they will **beat to a greater volume.**

This is because the cell walls are broken down by the water which turns to sharp ice crystals during freezing. Bring to room temperature before whisking.

45

If you ever find **you've over-salted a soup or stew,**

peel and slice a a raw potato, add to the pot and simmer gently until almost tender. The starch will absorb the excess salt and should then be discarded; add a little milk if further correction is needed.

46

Beurre manié

is one of the very best chef's tricks

for thickening sauces and casseroles at the last minute.

Work together equal amounts of soft butter and plain flour. Roll into small balls and drop singly into a gently simmering liquid and whisk in until sufficiently thickened. Allow to cook for several minutes.

47

Always store un-popped **popcorn** kernels in the freezer and pop from frozen. Amazingly, you will find that the corn will quickly pop and the rapid change in temperature will cause each of the kernels to pop larger than usual,

with much fluffier results.

48

a joint of **beef,** scatter some dry English **mustard powder** over the fat on the top. This **will bring out the full flavour** of the meat. You can also try a little Madras curry powder or Garam Masala. While roasting, the mustard and curry flavours amazingly fade away after curiously enhancing the true beef flavour.

49

When cooking a steamed pudding, place a few marbles in the pan containing the simmering water.

Their eventual **rattling will alert you** when the water is boiling dry and requires topping up. If using a plain aluminium pan, add some lemon juice to the water to prevent discolouration.

50

When making Irish coffees, there's a simple scientific secret worth knowing to **make the cream** float successfully. It is essential to dissolve a spoonful of sugar in the hot coffee first as this alters its density, allowing you to pour lightly whipped cream carefully over the back of a spoon so that it will **float on your coffee.**

Richard Maggs

A dynamic and accomplished chef, Richard Maggs has worked in many restaurants and hotels and was Manager of a three-star hotel by the age of 22. He has appeared on TV and radio, and is a regular columnist for a number of magazines including the prestigious *Aga Magazine*. A best-selling author, he is also the resident cookery expert, The Cookery Doctor, with the award-winning Agalinks website at www.agalinks.com. This is his eighth book.

THE LITTLE BOOK OF
BARBECUE
TIPS
ANDREW LANGLEY

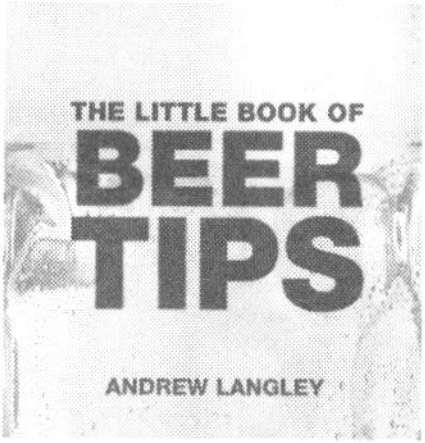
THE LITTLE BOOK OF
BEER
TIPS
ANDREW LANGLEY

THE LITTLE BOOK O
HER
TIPS
WILLIAM FORTT

THE LITTLE BOOK OF
POKER
TIPS
DAVID MITCHELL

THE LITTLE BOOK OF
GARDENING
TIPS
WILLIAM FORTT

THE LITTLE BOOK O
CHEFS'
TIPS
RICHARD MAGGS

THE LITTLE BOOK OF
SPICE
TIPS
ANDREW LANGLEY

THE LITTLE BOOK OF
GOLF
TIPS
PAUL HART

THE LITTLE BOOK O
TIPS
SERIES

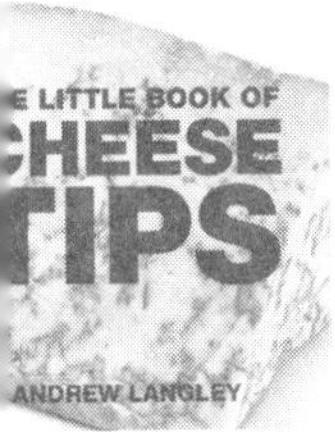

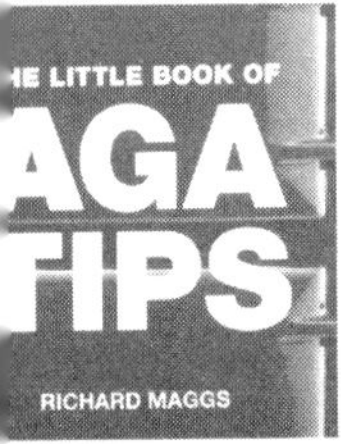

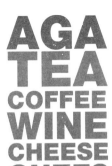

AGA
TEA
COFFEE
WINE
CHEESE
CHEFS
BARBECUE
HERB
GARDENING
SPICE
BEER
GOLF
POKER

Little Books of Tips from Absolute Press

The Little Book of Tea Tips
The Little Book of Wine Tips
The Little Book of Cheese Tips
The Little Book of Coffee Tips
The Little Book of Herb Tips
The Little Book of Gardening Tips
The Little Book of Barbecue Tips
The Little Book of Chefs' Tips
The Little Book of Spice Tips
The Little Book of Beer Tips
The Little Book of Poker Tips
The Little Book of Golf Tips
The Little Book of Aga Tips
The Little Book of Aga Tips 2
The Little Book of Aga Tips 3
The Little Book of Christmas Aga Tips
The Little Book of Rayburn Tips

Forthcoming titles:

The Little Book of Champagne Tips
The Little Book of Travel Tips
The Little Book of Cleaning Tips
The Little Book of Chocolate Tips
The Little Book of Diet Tips
The Little Book of Marmite Tips
The Little Book of Garden Design Tips
The Little Book of Container Plant Tips
The Little Book of Camping Tips
The Little Book of Puppy Tips
The Little Book of Kitten Tips

All titles: £2.99 / 112 pages

Acknowledgements

My thanks to all my family, friends, colleagues and fellow chefs everywhere for their constant support and encouragement. Special thanks to Ken and Carwen for their meticulous help in turning a pile of hastily-written notes into a manuscript while I was away working in Australia and New Zealand. Also a huge thank you to Jon, Matt and Meg at Absolute Press, they are everything a busy author could want – efficient, good fun to work with and lovers of great food.